So You Want To Be A Mental Health Professional

by
Dr. Roberto Jimenez
Licensed Mental Health Professional

DR. ROBERTO

From the Hero Author

Welcome, everyone!

My name is **Dr. Roberto Jimenez**. I am a *Psychotherapist* with **more than** *20 years of clinical experience* treating children and adults. I am a qualified MFT supervisor with over 20 years of clinical experience, and my approach to clients is eclectic, tailored to their unique needs, and wants. I work with individuals, couples, families, children, teenagers, the elderly, and LGBTQ. Manifest Your Best Life is a quick, easy-to-follow book helping individuals understand the manifestation process, from reviewing our thoughts, feelings, beliefs, and work ethics to bringing our dreams into reality. It's time to manifest your best life!

I am licensed in the following places:
- Licensed Marriage & Family Therapist in FL (MT1984)
- Licensed Mental Health Counselor in FL (MH10038)
- Independent Marriage & Family Therapist in Ohio - IMFT (F.2200249)
- Licensed Professional Counselor – LPC in Puerto Rico (4568)
- Licensed Marriage & Family Therapist - LMFT in North Carolina (2390)
- Licensed Marriage & Family Therapist - LMFT in Arkansas - (M2210004)
- Licensed Professional Counselor - LPC in Arkansas (P2210018)
- Licensed Marriage & Family Therapist - LMFT in California (Passed, pending activation)
- Licensed Marriage & Family Therapist - LMFT in New Jersey (Passed, pending activation)
- Licensed Marriage & Family Therapist - LMFT in Guam (MFT-027)
- Marriage & Family Therapist - LMFT in Minnesota (Taking the Legal and Ethics Exam in 2023)

Table of Contents

Introduction

Congratulations to all middle and high school students who are considering a career in mental health! It takes a lot of courage and empathy to pursue this field, and you should be proud of yourselves for thinking about making a positive impact on others. Mental health professionals play a critical role in helping people overcome challenges, improve their well-being, and lead fulfilling lives. As a mental health professional, you will have the opportunity to work with a diverse group of individuals, including children, teens, adults, and families. You will also get to help people struggling with a variety of issues, such as anxiety, depression, trauma, and relationship problems. The work can be challenging, but it can also be incredibly rewarding.

In order to become a mental health professional, you will need to complete a specific education and training program. This may include earning a bachelor's or master's degree in psychology, counseling, or a related field, as well as obtaining a license or certification. It is also important to develop strong communication, active listening, and problem-solving skills. In addition to your formal education, you may also gain valuable experience by volunteering or interning at a mental health clinic, hospital, or community center. This will give you the chance to work with clients, observe mental health professionals in action, and build your skills and knowledge.

I encourage you to continue learning about this exciting and meaningful field. Whether you become a psychologist, counselor, social worker, or another type of mental health professional, you will have the opportunity to make a difference in the lives of others every day. Remember, your empathy, compassion, and dedication will be your greatest assets as you pursue this career. Once again, congratulations on your consideration of this rewarding path, and I wish you all the best in your future endeavors!

Making the Decision and Planning

Becoming a mental health professional is a rewarding and challenging process that requires dedication, hard work, and a commitment to helping others. If you are interested in pursuing a career in this field, here is a step-by-step guide on how to become a mental health professional.

Step 01: Choose your career path.

The first step in becoming a mental health professional is to choose a specific career path. There are many different mental health professions, each with its own unique set of requirements, responsibilities, and specialties. Some of the most common mental health careers include:

- Clinical Psychologist
- Licensed Clinical Social Worker

- Licensed Professional Counselor
- Psychiatrist
- Marriage and Family Therapist

It is important to research each of these careers and their requirements to determine which one is the best fit for you. Consider your skills, interests, and desired work environment when making your decision.

Step 02: Get an education.

Once you have chosen your career path, the next step is to get the required education. For most mental health professions, this will require obtaining a graduate degree, such as a Master's or Doctorate degree. Some professions, such as clinical psychologists, also require additional post-doctoral training. Be sure to research the specific educational requirements for your chosen career path, and find a reputable program that meets those requirements.

Step 03: Gain practical experience.

In addition to formal education, it is also important to gain practical experience in the field. Many graduate programs offer opportunities for internships, practicums, and fieldwork, which provide hands-on experience working with clients and other mental health professionals. This experience will help you develop your skills and gain a deeper understanding of the field.

Step 04: Obtain licensure.

Once you have completed your education and gained practical experience, the next step is to obtain licensure. Licensure is required for most mental health professions and is usually obtained through the state in which you plan to practice. Requirements for licensure vary by state and by profession, but typically include passing a licensing exam and meeting a minimum number of supervised clinical hours.

Step 05: Stay current and improve your skills.

Continuing education and professional development is an important part of a successful mental health career. Keeping up with new research and advances in the field, attending conferences and workshops, and pursuing ongoing training opportunities will help you stay current and improve your skills.

Step 06: Build a network and seek support.

Building a network of other mental health professionals and seeking support from mentors can be incredibly valuable as you begin your career. These connections can provide you with professional guidance and support, as well as opportunities for collaboration and growth. Becoming a mental health professional is a challenging and rewarding process that requires dedication, hard work, and a commitment to helping others. By choosing a career path, obtaining an education, gaining practical experience, obtaining licensure, staying current, and building a network, you can achieve your goal of becoming a successful mental health professional.

The Field of Mental Health

Mental health refers to the psychological and emotional well-being of an individual. It is a complex and dynamic field that encompasses the study of the mind, emotions, and behavior, as well as the diagnosis, treatment, and prevention of mental illness and disorders. Mental health professionals work to help individuals achieve and maintain optimal mental and emotional health, and to help those who are struggling with mental illness or disorders. The field of mental health includes a wide range of professionals, including psychologists, psychiatrists, social workers, counseling professionals, and psychiatric nurses. These professionals use a variety of approaches, including psychotherapy, medication management, and support groups, to help individuals improve their mental health and well-being.

One of the key challenges in mental health is the stigma that still surrounds mental illness and disorders. Despite advances in research and treatment, many individuals are still reluctant to seek help for mental health problems due to the shame and embarrassment often associated with mental illness. This stigma can make it difficult for individuals to access the help they need and can also prevent mental health professionals from providing the care and support that individuals need. Another challenge in the field of mental health is the shortage of mental health professionals. This shortage can make it difficult for individuals to access the care they need, and can also put additional strain on mental health professionals who are already overworked and under-resourced. In addition, mental health professionals face a constant demand for training and continuing education to stay current on new developments in the field.

Despite these challenges, the field of mental health is

incredibly rewarding. Mental health professionals have the opportunity to make a positive impact in the lives of individuals, families, and communities. They help individuals overcome mental health problems, improve their relationships, and lead more fulfilling lives. They also work to reduce the burden of mental illness and improve access to mental health services for all individuals, regardless of their financial resources or social status. The field of mental health is an important and dynamic area of study and practice. Mental health professionals play a critical role in helping individuals improve their mental health and well-being, and in addressing the challenges and stigmas associated with mental illness and disorders. By working together, mental health professionals can help individuals achieve optimal mental and emotional health, and create a world in which mental health is valued and supported.

The Importance of Mental Health Professionals

Mental health professionals play a crucial role in promoting and maintaining the emotional, psychological, and behavioral well-being of individuals. Mental health is an essential component of overall health, and mental health professionals help individuals achieve and maintain a balanced state of mind and emotional stability. Mental health professionals provide a variety of services, including therapy, counseling, and psychiatric treatment. They work with individuals, families, and communities to help them better understand, manage, and overcome emotional, psychological, and behavioral issues. Mental health professionals provide support and guidance to help individuals work through their emotions and improve their emotional well-being. They can help individuals develop coping strategies to manage stress, anxiety, and depression, as well as identify and address the underlying causes of these conditions.

Mental health professionals can help individuals improve their interpersonal relationships by teaching them effective communication skills, conflict resolution strategies, and problem-solving skills. They can also help individuals work through relationship issues and improve their ability to form and maintain healthy relationships. Mental health professionals can help individuals develop resilience and the ability to cope with life's challenges. By providing individuals with the tools they need to manage stress, overcome adversity, and bounce back from setbacks, mental health professionals can help individuals become stronger and more resilient.

Mental health professionals can also help individuals gain a deeper understanding of themselves and their thoughts, feelings, and behaviors. They can provide guidance and support as individuals work through personal issues and develop a better sense of self. By addressing emotional, psychological, and behavioral issues, mental health professionals can help individuals improve their overall quality of life. They can help individuals feel happier, more confident, and more fulfilled, and can provide support as individuals work towards their personal goals.

Mental health professionals also play an important role in addressing the mental health needs of communities and populations. They can work with schools, businesses, and community organizations to promote mental health awareness, prevent mental health problems, and provide early intervention services to those in need. By working with communities, mental health professionals can help create supportive environments that promote mental well-being and reduce the stigma associated with mental health issues. Mental health professionals are essential in promoting and maintaining the emotional, psychological, and behavioral well-being of individuals and communities. By providing a range of services, including therapy, counseling, and psychiatric treatment, mental health professionals help individuals work through their emotions, improve their relationships, and achieve a better quality of life. Additionally, by working with communities, mental health professionals can help create supportive environments that promote mental well-being and reduce the stigma associated with mental health issues.

Practitioner VS Researcher

While you do not have to decide now, it may be useful for you to begin considering whether you want to become a practitioner or researcher in the field of mental health. A practitioner is someone who practices in the field. For example, therapists are practitioners because they actually work directly with patients to improve their outcomes. In contrast, mental health researchers are the ones who conduct studies to better understand the human condition, mental health, and how to improve the therapies that people receive. Mental health therapy and mental health research are both important fields in the study of psychology and mental health, but they are quite different in their goals, methods, and approaches. Mental health therapy focuses on helping individuals improve their mental and emotional well-being, while mental health research focuses on understanding and explaining mental processes and disorders.

Mental health therapists, such as psychologists, social workers, and counselors, work directly with individuals to help them overcome mental health problems and achieve greater well-being. They use a variety of techniques, including psychotherapy, support groups, and medication management, to help individuals improve their mental and emotional health. Mental health therapists work one-on-one with individuals, and they are trained to help individuals understand their thoughts and

Dr. Roberto Jimenez • *So You Want To Be A Mental Health Professional*

emotions, and to provide support and guidance to help individuals overcome mental health problems. Mental health researchers, on the other hand, focus on understanding the underlying causes of mental health problems, and on developing and testing new treatments and interventions. Mental health researchers often work in academic settings, such as universities or research institutions, and they use a variety of methods, including experiments, surveys, and case studies, to gather data and test theories about mental health and disorders. Mental health researchers are also involved in developing and testing new treatments, such as medications or therapies, that may be used to help individuals overcome mental health problems.

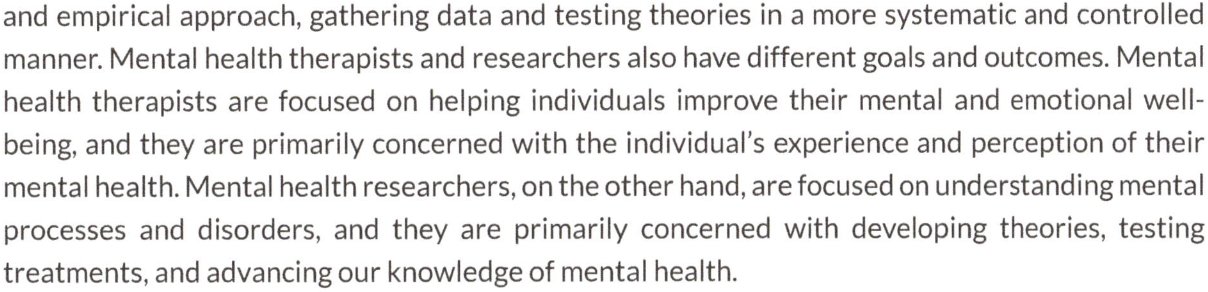

The approaches and methods used by mental health therapists and researchers are also quite different. Mental health therapists use a more subjective and experiential approach, focusing on the individual's subjective experience of mental health problems and seeking to understand their perspective and experiences. Mental health researchers, on the other hand, use a more objective and empirical approach, gathering data and testing theories in a more systematic and controlled manner. Mental health therapists and researchers also have different goals and outcomes. Mental health therapists are focused on helping individuals improve their mental and emotional well-being, and they are primarily concerned with the individual's experience and perception of their mental health. Mental health researchers, on the other hand, are focused on understanding mental processes and disorders, and they are primarily concerned with developing theories, testing treatments, and advancing our knowledge of mental health.

Despite these differences, mental health therapy and mental health research are both critical to the study of psychology and mental health, and they both play important roles in improving the lives of individuals with mental health problems. Mental health therapy provides individuals with the support and guidance they need to overcome mental health problems and achieve greater well-being, while mental health research helps us better understand the underlying causes of mental health problems and develop new and effective treatments. Mental health therapy and mental health research are both important and distinct fields in the study of psychology and mental health. Mental health therapists work directly with individuals to help them improve their mental and emotional well-being, while mental health researchers focus on understanding and explaining mental processes and disorders. By working together, mental health therapists and researchers can help individuals overcome mental health problems and achieve greater well-being, and contribute to the advancement of our knowledge and understanding of mental health.

Psychiatrists

Description and Overview

A psychiatrist is a medical doctor who specializes in the treatment of mental illness and emotional disorders. They are trained to diagnose and treat mental health problems, and they play a crucial role in helping individuals overcome mental health problems and achieve greater well-being. The role of a psychiatrist involves a combination of medical and therapeutic treatments. Psychiatrists use a variety of techniques, including psychotherapy, medication management, and behavioral therapy, to help individuals overcome mental health problems. They are also trained to perform physical exams and order lab tests to help diagnose mental health problems and determine the best course of treatment. One of the key responsibilities of a psychiatrist is to diagnose mental health problems. This involves evaluating an individual's symptoms, medical history, and life circumstances to determine the underlying cause of their mental health problems. Psychiatrists use a variety of diagnostic tools and techniques, including standardized tests, interviews, and observations, to gather information about an individual's mental health. They then use this information to make a diagnosis and develop a treatment plan.

Once a diagnosis has been made, psychiatrists work with individuals to develop a treatment plan. This may involve a combination of psychotherapy, medication, and behavioral therapies.

 Dr. Roberto Jimenez • *So You Want To Be A Mental Health Professional*

Psychotherapy involves talking with individuals about their thoughts, emotions, and experiences, and helping them understand and overcome mental health problems. Medication management involves prescribing and monitoring the use of psychiatric medications to help alleviate symptoms and improve mental health. Behavioral therapy involves working with individuals to modify their behavior and thoughts to help improve their mental health. In addition to providing direct treatment to individuals, psychiatrists also play a critical role in helping individuals access the resources they need to overcome mental health problems. This may involve making referrals to community resources, such as support groups or community mental health services, or working with families and caregivers to ensure that individuals receive the support they need.

Another important aspect of the job of a psychiatrist is research. Psychiatrists often conduct research to better understand the underlying causes of mental health problems and to develop new and effective treatments. They may also participate in clinical trials to test new treatments and interventions. In order to become a psychiatrist, individuals must first complete a bachelor's degree and then go on to earn a medical degree from an accredited medical school. After medical school, individuals must complete a residency in psychiatry, during which they receive intensive training in the diagnosis and treatment of mental health problems. In addition, many states require psychiatrists to be licensed and to pass a certification exam in order to practice. Being a psychiatrist can be both rewarding and challenging. On one hand, psychiatrists have the opportunity to make a real difference in the lives of individuals with mental health problems, helping them overcome their problems and achieve greater well-being. On the other hand, working with individuals with mental health problems can be emotionally demanding, and psychiatrists must be able to manage the stress and emotional demands of their job.

Psychiatrist are trained to diagnose and treat mental health problems, and they use a combination of medical and therapeutic treatments to help individuals overcome mental health problems and achieve greater well-being. The job of a psychiatrist is both rewarding and challenging, and it requires extensive training, education, and experience. However, for those who are passionate about helping individuals with mental health problems, it can be a fulfilling and meaningful career.

Steps to Becoming a Psychiatrist

Becoming a psychiatrist in the United States requires a significant investment of time, energy, and resources. However, for those who are passionate about helping individuals with mental health problems, the rewards of a career in psychiatry can be both fulfilling and rewarding. The first step in becoming a psychiatrist is to earn a bachelor's degree. While there is no specific major required to become a psychiatrist, many individuals choose to major in a field such as psychology, biology, or neuroscience to gain a strong foundation in the sciences and to develop the critical thinking and problem-solving skills that are necessary for success in the field. After earning a bachelor's degree, individuals must then go on to earn a medical degree from an accredited medical school.

This typically takes four years and involves extensive coursework in the sciences, as well as clinical rotations in a variety of medical specialties.

Once an individual has completed medical school, they must then complete a residency in psychiatry. Residencies in psychiatry typically last four years and provide intensive training in the diagnosis and treatment of mental health problems. During residency, individuals work with patients in a variety of settings, including hospitals, clinics, and community mental health centers, to gain practical experience diagnosing and treating mental health problems. After completing residency, individuals must then be licensed to practice psychiatry in the United States. To be licensed, individuals must pass the United States Medical Licensing Examination (USMLE) and meet the licensing requirements of the state in which they plan to practice. These requirements may include passing additional exams and completing continuing education courses.

In addition to being licensed, many psychiatrists choose to become certified by the American Board of Psychiatry and Neurology (ABPN). The ABPN certifies individuals who have completed the necessary education and training, and who have demonstrated their expertise in the field of psychiatry. Becoming certified by the ABPN is optional, but it can help individuals establish their credibility and competitiveness in the field. Once individuals have completed the necessary education and training, they are then ready to begin practicing psychiatry. The specific duties of a psychiatrist will depend on their area of specialization and the type of patients they see, but in general, they are responsible for diagnosing and treating mental health problems, prescribing medications, and working with patients to develop treatment plans. They may also conduct research, participate in clinical trials, and make referrals to community resources as needed.

Working as a psychiatrist can be highly fulfilling. On one hand, psychiatrists have the opportunity to make a real difference in the lives of individuals with mental health problems, helping them overcome their problems and achieve greater well-being. On the other hand, working with individuals with mental health problems can be emotionally demanding, and psychiatrists must be able to manage the stress and emotional demands of their job. Becoming a psychiatrist in the United States requires a significant investment of time, energy, and resources. Individuals must first earn a bachelor's degree, then go on to earn a medical degree from an accredited medical school, complete a residency in psychiatry, and be licensed to practice psychiatry in the United States. Working as a psychiatrist can be both challenging and rewarding, but for those who are passionate about helping individuals with mental health problems, it can be a fulfilling and meaningful career.

  Dr. Roberto Jimenez • *So You Want To Be A Mental Health Professional*

Psychologists

Description and Overview

Psychologists are mental health professionals who use their training and expertise to help individuals, families, and organizations better understand and address a wide range of psychological issues and problems. They use a variety of techniques and methods to assess, diagnose, and treat individuals with mental health problems, as well as to promote psychological well-being and improve the quality of life for those they serve. The specific responsibilities of psychologists can vary widely depending on their area of specialization and the setting in which they work. Psychologists use a variety of methods to assess individuals' mental and emotional functioning, including standardized tests, behavioral observation, and structured interviews. They may also gather information from family members, medical records, and other sources to gain a complete understanding of an individual's mental health problems.

Psychologists use their training and expertise to diagnose mental health problems, such as depression, anxiety, and schizophrenia. They may use the criteria outlined in the Diagnostic and Statistical Manual of Mental Disorders (DSM) to make these diagnoses. Based on their assessments and diagnoses, psychologists work with individuals to develop treatment plans that are tailored to their specific needs and goals. Treatment plans may involve a combination of psychotherapy, medication, and other interventions, such as life skills training or coping strategies. Psychologists use a variety of therapeutic approaches to help individuals address their mental health problems and improve their overall well-being. These approaches may include cognitive-behavioral therapy (CBT), dialectical behavioral therapy (DBT), and humanistic therapy, among others.

In some states, psychologists are authorized to prescribe medication. In these states, they may use their expertise in mental health to assess individuals' needs for medication and to make appropriate prescriptions. Many psychologists are also engaged in research to better understand the causes of mental health problems and to develop new and more effective treatments. This may involve conducting experimental studies, analyzing data, and writing reports and articles for publication. Psychologists often work with other mental health professionals, such as social workers, counselors, and psychiatrists, to provide comprehensive and coordinated care for individuals with mental health problems. They may also consult with schools, businesses, and other organizations to help them address psychological issues and promote a positive work environment.

The specific requirements for becoming a psychologist vary by state, but in general, individuals must have a master's or doctoral degree in psychology from an accredited institution. They must also complete an internship or supervised professional practice, and pass a licensing exam in order to practice psychology in their state. Some states also require continuing education and/or certification from a professional organization, such as the American Psychological Association (APA). Working as a psychologist can be both challenging and rewarding. On one hand, psychologists have the opportunity to make a real difference in the lives of individuals with mental health problems, helping them overcome their problems and achieve greater well-being. On the other hand, working with individuals with mental health problems can be emotionally demanding, and psychologists must be able to manage the stress and emotional demands of their job. They use a variety of techniques and methods to assess, diagnose, and treat individuals with mental health problems, and to promote psychological well-being and improve the quality of life for those they serve. Becoming a psychologist typically requires a master's or doctoral degree in psychology, and completion of an internship.

Steps to Become a Psychologist

Becoming a psychologist in the United States requires a significant amount of education, training, and professional experience. Here are the basic steps to becoming a licensed psychologist:

- Earn a bachelor's degree: The first step in becoming a psychologist is to earn a bachelor's degree in psychology or a related field, such as sociology or neuroscience. This degree provides a foundation in the principles and theories of psychology, as well as a broad understanding of the social sciences.
- Obtain a master's or doctoral degree in psychology: After completing a bachelor's degree, individuals must pursue a master's or doctoral degree in psychology from an accredited program.

     Dr. Roberto Jimenez • *So You Want To Be A Mental Health Professional*

Doctoral programs in psychology typically take five to seven years to complete and include coursework in advanced psychology theories, research methods, and clinical practice. During this time, students may also complete an internship or practicum to gain hands-on experience in a real-world setting.

- Complete supervised professional practice: After completing a doctoral degree, individuals must complete a period of supervised professional practice, also known as a postdoctoral residency. During this time, psychologists work under the supervision of a licensed psychologist, providing psychological services and honing their clinical skills. The length of this period varies by state but is typically between 1,500 and 2,000 hours.
- Pass a licensing exam: After completing a postdoctoral residency, individuals must pass a licensing exam to become licensed psychologists in their state. The most widely used licensing exam in the United States is the Examination for Professional Practice in Psychology (EPPP), which tests an individual's knowledge of psychology and their ability to practice competently and ethically.
- Meet continuing education requirements: Psychologists are typically required to participate in ongoing professional development activities and complete continuing education credits to maintain their license. This helps ensure that psychologists stay up-to-date with the latest research and practices in the field.

In addition to these basic requirements, individuals interested in becoming psychologists may also choose to pursue specialty certifications, such as certification in cognitive behavioral therapy or psychoanalytic psychotherapy. These certifications can help psychologists demonstrate their expertise in specific areas and improve their job prospects. It's also important to note that the requirements for becoming a psychologist vary by state. While many states have similar requirements, some states have additional requirements, such as additional coursework, exams, or supervised professional practice hours. Individuals interested in becoming psychologists should familiarize themselves with the requirements in their state and consider obtaining licensure in multiple states if they plan to practice in more than one location. Becoming a psychologist in the United States requires a significant investment of time and resources, including a bachelor's degree, a master's or doctoral degree in psychology, a postdoctoral residency, a licensing exam, and ongoing professional development. However, for individuals who are passionate about helping others and have a strong interest in psychology, the rewards of this career can be substantial, both personally and professionally.

Mental Health Counselors

Description and Overview

A mental health counselor is a professional trained to help individuals who are experiencing emotional, psychological, and behavioral difficulties. They work with clients to help them understand and manage their thoughts, feelings, and behaviors, and to develop coping skills for dealing with life's challenges. Mental health counselors may work in a variety of settings, including community mental health centers, hospitals, schools, private practices, and government agencies. The role of a mental health counselor is to provide support and guidance to individuals struggling with mental health issues. This may involve working with clients who have been diagnosed with conditions such as depression, anxiety, bipolar disorder, and post-traumatic stress disorder (PTSD). Mental health counselors also work with clients who are dealing with relationship problems, stress, and other emotional difficulties. They use a variety of therapeutic techniques to help clients gain insight into their thoughts and feelings, and to identify patterns of behavior that may be contributing to their difficulties.

One of the primary duties of a mental health counselor is to conduct assessments of clients. This may involve gathering information about the client's medical history, family background, and current living situation. The counselor may also use standardized tests and other tools to gather information about the client's mental health and well-being. Based on the results of the assessment, the counselor will develop a treatment plan to help the client achieve their goals. Once a treatment plan is in place, mental health counselors work with clients to help them understand and manage their thoughts, feelings, and behaviors. This may involve teaching them coping skills, such as relaxation techniques and problem-solving strategies, to help them deal with difficult situations. Mental health counselors may also help clients explore their feelings and thoughts, and to identify and challenge negative beliefs and thought patterns. In addition to providing individual therapy, mental health counselors may also facilitate group therapy sessions. These sessions provide a supportive environment where clients can share their experiences and support one another. Group therapy is often used to help clients who are dealing with similar issues, such as addiction or trauma. It can also be an effective way for clients to develop social skills and to learn from one another.

Another important aspect of a mental health counselor's job is to collaborate with other healthcare professionals to provide comprehensive care to clients. For example, a mental health counselor may work with a physician or psychiatrist to develop a medication plan for a client with a mental illness. They may also work with teachers and other school personnel to support students who are struggling with emotional and behavioral difficulties. Mental health counselors also play an important role in advocating for their clients and promoting mental health awareness. This may involve working with community organizations, schools, and government agencies to raise awareness about mental health issues and to promote access to mental health services. Mental health counselors may also participate in research projects to advance the field of mental health and to develop new and effective treatments for mental illness.

Finally, mental health counselors must adhere to ethical and professional standards in their work. This includes maintaining client confidentiality, avoiding conflicts of interest, and avoiding harm to clients. Mental health counselors also need to be familiar with laws and regulations governing mental health care, such as the Health Insurance Portability and Accountability Act (HIPAA). The job of a mental health counselor can be highly rewarding. Mental health counselors play an important role in helping individuals who are struggling with mental health issues, and in promoting mental health awareness and access to mental health services. To be effective in this role, mental health counselors must have strong interpersonal and communication skills, a deep understanding

of human behavior and psychology, and a commitment to ethical and professional standards.

Steps to Become a Mental Health Counselor

Becoming a mental health counselor requires a combination of education, training, and professional experience. The following steps outline the process of becoming a mental health counselor:

- Earn a bachelor's degree: A bachelor's degree in psychology, counseling, or a related field is usually the first step in becoming a mental health counselor. A bachelor's degree provides a foundation in the theories and principles of psychology and human behavior, as well as an understanding of research methods and statistics. Some bachelor's degree programs offer the opportunity to gain hands-on experience through internships or practicums.

- Gain work experience: While not always required, gaining work experience in a related field can be helpful in developing skills and knowledge that are relevant to mental health counseling. This might include working in a social service agency, a mental health clinic, or a school.
- Complete a master's degree: A master's degree in counseling, psychology, or a related field is typically the minimum requirement for becoming a licensed mental health counselor. During a master's program, students take courses in human development, abnormal psychology, and the theories and techniques of counseling. They also complete a supervised internship or practicum, which provides hands-on experience working with clients.
- Obtain licensure: After completing a master's degree, mental health counselors must obtain a license in order to practice legally. Licensing requirements vary by state, but typically include passing a standardized exam and meeting requirements for continuing education. The National Board for Certified Counselors (NBCC) offers the National Counselor Examination for Licensure and Certification (NCE), which is recognized by many states as a licensure exam.
- Gain professional experience: After obtaining a license, mental health counselors typically work in a supervised setting, such as a mental health clinic, school, or private practice. During this time, they gain experience working with clients, developing treatment plans, and using therapeutic techniques. Some states require a certain number of hours of supervised experience before mental health counselors can practice independently.
- Maintain professional development: Mental health counselors must engage in continuing education and professional development in order to maintain their licensure. This may include attending conferences and workshops, participating in continuing education courses, and engaging in professional networking.
- Specialize in a particular area: Mental health counselors may choose to specialize in a particular area, such as working with children, couples, or individuals with specific mental health conditions. Specialization may require additional education and training, as well as professional experience.

Becoming a mental health counselor requires a combination of education, training, and professional experience. The process typically involves earning a bachelor's degree, gaining work experience, completing a master's degree, obtaining licensure, gaining professional experience, maintaining professional development, and potentially specializing in a particular area. Mental health counselors must be dedicated to helping others and have strong interpersonal and communication skills, as well as a deep understanding of human behavior and psychology.

Social Workers

Description and Overview

Social workers play a crucial role in helping individuals, families, and communities navigate complex social and psychological issues. They work in a variety of settings, including schools, hospitals, government agencies, and non-profit organizations. Social workers help clients access resources, advocate for their rights, and provide support as they navigate life's challenges. Social workers assess the needs of clients, taking into consideration their individual circumstances, environment, and relationships. They identify any issues that may be contributing to a client's difficulties and develop a plan of action to help them. Social workers help clients access the resources and services they need to improve their situation. This may involve connecting them with government programs, community organizations, or other support services. Social workers also help clients navigate complex systems, such as the healthcare system, and advocate for their rights.

Social workers provide counseling and support to clients as they work through their problems. They use a range of therapeutic techniques, including individual and group therapy, to help clients improve their mental health and well-being.

Social workers advocate for clients, particularly those who may be marginalized or facing discrimination. They work to ensure that their clients receive fair treatment and access to necessary resources and services. Social workers often collaborate with other professionals, such as doctors, teachers, and lawyers, to provide comprehensive support to their clients. They coordinate with these professionals to develop integrated treatment plans and ensure that their clients receive the best possible care.

Social workers maintain accurate and confidential records of their clients' cases, documenting their progress and any interventions or treatments provided. These records are used to monitor the effectiveness of interventions and to inform future decision-making. Social workers are involved in research and evaluation to improve the services and interventions they provide. They collect data on the effectiveness of their interventions, analyze it, and use it to inform their practice. To become a social worker, individuals typically need to earn a bachelor's degree in social work (BSW) or a master's degree in social work (MSW). A BSW provides a foundation in the theories and principles of social work, while an MSW provides more advanced training in clinical social work, research, and policy analysis. Many states also require social workers to be licensed, which typically involves passing an exam and meeting requirements for continuing education.

Social workers must have strong interpersonal and communication skills, as well as the ability to think critically and creatively. They must be compassionate, empathetic, and dedicated to helping others. They must also be able to manage their own emotions and maintain professional boundaries, as their work can be emotionally challenging. Social workers play a vital role in helping individuals, families, and communities navigate complex social and psychological issues. Their job involves assessment, case management, counseling, advocacy, collaboration, record-keeping, and research and evaluation. To become a social worker, individuals typically need to earn a bachelor's or master's degree in social work, and obtain licensure in their state. Social workers must have strong interpersonal and communication skills, as well as the ability to manage their emotions and maintain professional boundaries.

Steps to Become a Social Worker

Becoming a social worker requires a combination of education, training, and hands-on experience. This comprehensive guide will outline the steps necessary to pursue a career in social work, including the following:

- Earn a bachelor's degree in social work (BSW): A BSW program provides a foundation in the theories and principles of social work. It typically includes coursework in subjects such as human behavior and the social environment, social welfare policy and services, and research methods. BSW programs also typically include a field placement, which provides hands-on experience in a social work setting.
- Gain experience: Some employers prefer to hire social workers with prior experience in a related field, such as human services, healthcare, or education. While earning a BSW, consider volunteering or working part-time in a social service agency to gain relevant experience.
- Consider obtaining a master's degree in social work (MSW): While a BSW is the minimum requirement for many entry-level social work positions, an MSW can provide more advanced

training in clinical social work, research, and policy analysis. It can also increase job opportunities and earning potential.

- Complete field placement: Most MSW programs include a field placement, which provides hands-on experience in a social work setting. Field placements provide an opportunity to apply what was learned in the classroom to real-world situations, and to build professional relationships with experienced social workers.
- Pass the required licensing exam: Social workers must be licensed in most states to practice. Requirements for licensure vary by state, but typically include passing a written exam and meeting continuing education requirements.
- Maintain professional competence: Social workers are expected to maintain professional competence throughout their careers, which often includes completing continuing education courses and participating in professional development opportunities.
- Consider specialized training: Some social workers choose to specialize in a particular area of practice, such as clinical social work, school social work, or geriatric social work. Specialized training and experience can increase job opportunities and earning potential.

There are several key qualities that can help individuals succeed as social workers. These include strong interpersonal and communication skills, empathy, compassion, and the ability to think critically and creatively. Social workers must also be able to manage their own emotions and maintain professional boundaries, as their work can be emotionally challenging. Once the steps to becoming a social worker have been completed, individuals will be well-positioned to pursue a rewarding and fulfilling career helping others. Social workers play a crucial role in helping individuals, families, and communities navigate complex social and psychological issues. They work in a variety of settings, including schools, hospitals, government agencies, and non-profit organizations, and help clients access resources, advocate for their rights, and provide support as they navigate life's challenges.

Becoming a social worker requires a combination of education, training, and hands-on experience. Individuals must earn a bachelor's degree in social work, gain relevant experience, consider obtaining a master's degree, complete field placement, pass the required licensing exam, maintain professional competence, and consider specialized training. Key qualities for success as a social worker include strong interpersonal and communication skills, empathy, compassion, and the ability to think critically and creatively. With the right combination of education, training, and experience, individuals can pursue a rewarding and fulfilling career as a social worker.

Marriage and Family Therapists

Description and Overview

A Marriage and Family Therapist (MFT) is a mental health professional who provides therapy to individuals, couples, and families to address a wide range of emotional and behavioral problems. MFTs help clients identify and resolve conflicts, improve communication, and strengthen relationships. The job of a MFT requires a combination of clinical skills, compassion, and a deep understanding of human relationships. The first step in therapy is to assess the client's needs and determine the best course of treatment. MFTs conduct thorough evaluations of individuals, couples, and families to gather information about their relationships, emotional and mental health, and other relevant factors. They use this information to make an accurate diagnosis and develop a treatment plan.

MFTs use a variety of therapy approaches, including cognitive-behavioral therapy, psychodynamic therapy, and family systems therapy, to help clients address their emotional and behavioral problems. They work with clients to identify the root causes of their problems and help them develop new coping skills and strategies. They may also work with couples to improve communication and resolve conflicts, or with families to address issues such as parent-child relationships, family dynamics, and substance abuse. In addition to working directly with clients, MFTs often collaborate with other mental health professionals, such as psychiatrists and psychologists, to provide comprehensive treatment. They may also work with medical doctors, school personnel, and community agencies to coordinate care and ensure clients receive the support they need. MFTs are responsible for maintaining accurate and confidential records of their clients' treatment. They document their assessments, treatment plans, progress notes, and any relevant information about their clients' health and well-being. Like all mental health professionals, MFTs must keep up-to-date with the latest developments in their field. They attend continuing education courses, conferences, and workshops to stay informed about new research, best practices, and emerging treatments.

MFTs must adhere to strict ethical standards and maintain client confidentiality. They must also be familiar with relevant laws and regulations, such as the Health Insurance Portability and Accountability Act (HIPAA), which governs the protection and confidentiality of client health information. To become an MFT, individuals must first earn a master's degree in counseling or a related field, such as psychology or social work. They must also complete a certain number of clinical hours under the supervision of a licensed therapist and pass a licensing exam. Some states also require MFTs to complete additional training in marriage and family therapy., MFTs must possess several key qualities that are essential for success in their field. These include strong communication and interpersonal skills, empathy, patience, and the ability to think critically and creatively. They must also be able to maintain professional boundaries, even in the face of emotional challenges, and to remain non-judgmental and respectful in their interactions with clients.

A Marriage and Family Therapist (MFT) is a mental health professional who provides therapy to individuals, couples, and families to address a wide range of emotional and behavioral problems. The job of a MFT requires a combination of clinical skills, compassion, and a deep understanding of human relationships. To become a MFT, individuals must earn a master's degree in counseling or a related field, complete clinical hours, pass a licensing exam, and maintain professional competence through continuing education and professional development. Key qualities for success as a MFT include strong communication and interpersonal skills, empathy, patience, and the ability to think critically and creatively. With the right combination of education, training, and experience, individuals can pursue a rewarding and fulfilling career as a MFT.

Steps to Become a Marriage and Family Therapist

Becoming a Marriage and Family Therapist (MFT) is a rewarding career path that requires dedication, compassion, and a deep understanding of human relationships. Here are the steps to become a MFT:

- Earn a Bachelor's Degree: The first step in becoming a MFT is to earn a bachelor's degree in a relevant field, such as psychology, sociology, or counseling. This degree provides a solid foundation in the social sciences, as well as an introduction to the theories and techniques used in therapy.
- Complete a Master's Degree: After earning a bachelor's degree, individuals must complete a master's degree in counseling, psychology, or a related field. This degree provides more in-depth training in the theories and techniques used in therapy, as well as hands-on experience working with clients.

- Gain Clinical Experience: Most states require MFTs to complete a certain number of clinical hours under the supervision of a licensed therapist before becoming licensed. This experience provides an opportunity to work with clients, observe experienced therapists, and develop the skills needed to be an effective therapist.
- Pass a Licensing Exam: After completing a master's degree and clinical hours, individuals must pass a licensing exam to become a licensed MFT. The exam typically covers topics such as ethics, diagnosis and treatment, and family systems.
- Maintain Professional Competence: To maintain their license, MFTs must complete continuing education courses and attend professional development workshops and conferences. This helps them stay up-to-date with the latest developments in their field and continue to grow as a therapist.
- Specialize in Marriage and Family Therapy: While some states require MFTs to complete additional training in marriage and family therapy, others do not. However, individuals who specialize in this area are better equipped to provide effective therapy to couples and families.
- Seek Supervision: New MFTs should seek supervision from an experienced therapist to help them navigate the challenges of their early career. Supervision provides an opportunity to receive feedback, discuss difficult cases, and grow as a therapist.

In addition to such formal requirements, MFTs must possess several key qualities that are essential for success in their field. These include strong communication and interpersonal skills, empathy, patience, and the ability to think critically and creatively. They must also be able to maintain professional boundaries, even in the face of emotional challenges, and to remain non-judgmental and respectful in their interactions with clients. Becoming an MFT is a challenging and rewarding process that requires a significant investment of time and effort. However, with the right combination of education, training, and experience, individuals can pursue a fulfilling career helping others to improve their relationships and their lives.

Certified Peer Specialists

Description and Overview

A Certified Peer Specialist (CPS) is an individual who has personal experience with mental illness, substance abuse, or both, and has been trained to use that experience to support others in their recovery journeys. As a CPS, they work with individuals who are experiencing mental health challenges and help them to develop the skills and strategies they need to live fulfilling lives. CPSs work with individuals to help them identify their personal goals and develop a plan to achieve them. They help clients to understand their mental health conditions, develop coping strategies, and access community resources that can support their recovery.

CPSs understand the importance of building trusting and supportive relationships with their clients. They listen to clients' concerns, respect their opinions, and work with them to develop solutions that are tailored to their unique needs and circumstances. CPSs help clients to become their own advocates, encouraging them to take an active role in their own care and treatment. They provide guidance and support as clients navigate the mental health system, and help them to understand their rights and responsibilities. CPSs draw on their own personal experiences to provide peer support to others. They use their understanding of the challenges and obstacles that individuals face in their recovery journeys to offer empathy, encouragement, and hope. CPSs work in collaboration with mental health providers, such as psychiatrists, psychologists, and therapists, to ensure that clients receive comprehensive and coordinated care. They serve as a liaison between clients and their mental health providers, and help to ensure that clients' needs and preferences are respected.

To become a CPS, individuals must complete a training program that includes both didactic and experiential components. The training covers topics such as mental health recovery, advocacy, peer support, and ethics. Additionally, individuals must pass a certification exam that assesses their knowledge and skills as a peer specialist. CPSs must also be able to demonstrate a strong commitment to their clients and to their own personal recovery. They must be able to maintain a positive and supportive attitude, even in the face of difficult circumstances, and to remain empathetic, patient, and understanding in their interactions with clients. The role of a CPS is to provide hope, support,

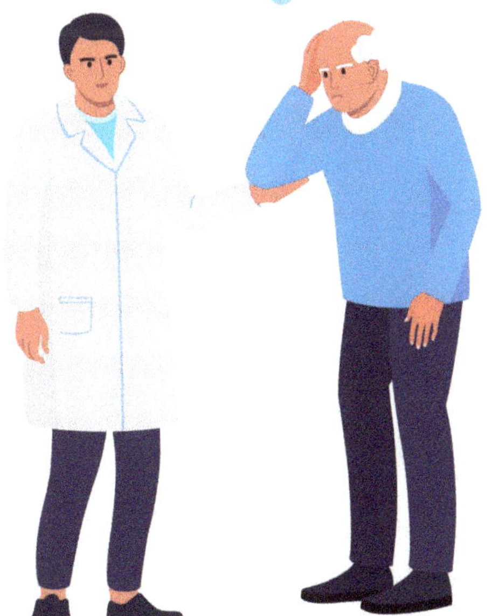

and empowerment to individuals who are facing mental health challenges. By drawing on their own experiences and training, they help clients to build the skills and strategies they need to live fulfilling and meaningful lives.

Steps to Become a Certified Peer Specialist

Becoming a Certified Peer Specialist (CPS) involves several steps, including education and training, passing a certification exam, and meeting ethical and professional standards. Here is a step-by-step guide to becoming a CPS:

- Meet Eligibility Requirements: Before you can become a CPS, you must meet certain eligibility requirements. These typically include having a personal experience with mental illness or substance abuse, being in recovery, and being able to demonstrate a commitment to supporting others in their recovery journeys.
- Complete a Training Program: To become a CPS, you must complete a training program that is approved by your state or jurisdiction. These programs typically include both didactic and experiential components, covering topics such as mental health recovery, advocacy, peer support, and ethics. Some programs may require that you have a certain level of education or experience, so it is important to check with your state or jurisdiction for specific requirements.
- Pass a Certification Exam: After completing a training program, you must pass a certification exam that assesses your knowledge and skills as a peer specialist. The exam will test your understanding of mental health recovery, peer support, ethics, and other relevant topics.
- Maintain Professional and Ethical Standards: To maintain your certification as a CPS, you must adhere to ethical and professional standards. This may include completing continuing education requirements, upholding standards of confidentiality and privacy, and avoiding conflicts of interest.
- Find Employment Opportunities: Once you have completed the steps above, you are ready to begin your career as a CPS. You can search for job opportunities through online job boards, professional associations, and mental health organizations. Many CPSs work in community-based mental health agencies, hospitals, or schools, while others work in private practices.

Becoming a CPS requires dedication, hard work, and a commitment to supporting others. By completing a training program, passing a certification exam, and meeting ethical and professional standards, you can become a valued member of the mental health community and help individuals to build the skills and strategies they need to live fulfilling lives.

Obtaining a College Degree

A college degree can open doors to many opportunities and provide a foundation for a successful career. For many junior high and high school students, the thought of pursuing a college degree can be both exciting and overwhelming. Junior high and high school students should start thinking about what they want to do in the future and what type of career they want to pursue. Research different careers and industries, talk to people in those fields, and attend college fairs to get a better understanding of what a college education can provide. It is important to set realistic and attainable goals for the future. Consider factors such as finances, personal interests, and academic abilities when setting these goals. It is also important to have a backup plan in case your initial goals change or do not work out.

Good grades and a strong academic record are important when applying to college. Take challenging classes, participate in extracurricular activities, and seek help from teachers and tutors if needed. It is also important to take standardized tests, such as the SAT or ACT, to demonstrate your abilities to colleges. There are many colleges to choose from, and it is important to find one that is a good fit. Research colleges based on their location, size, and programs offered, and consider factors such as cost, campus life, and accessibility. Make a list of colleges you are interested in and schedule campus visits to get a better understanding of what each college has to offer. College can be expensive, but there are many options for financial aid and scholarships. Start researching financial aid options early, including grants, scholarships, and student loans, and understand the different types of aid and how to apply for them. It is also important to think about how much debt you are willing to take on, and to plan accordingly.

Participating in community service and volunteer activities can help demonstrate your leadership and teamwork skills to colleges. It can also provide valuable experiences that can enhance your college application and help you stand out from other applicants. Talk to family members, friends, teachers, and guidance counselors to get advice on the college process. They may have valuable insights and can provide support and guidance as you navigate the college application process. When applying to colleges, it is important to follow the instructions carefully and provide accurate and complete information. Some colleges may also require essays, letters of recommendation, and transcripts, so be sure to ask for these items well in advance. For

some students, taking a gap year can provide valuable experiences and help them gain a better understanding of what they want to study in college. During this time, students can travel, work, or participate in volunteer activities to gain new perspectives and experiences.

College can be a big adjustment, so it is important to be prepared for the transition. Get involved in campus life, attend events, and meet new people to help you feel more comfortable. Additionally, make sure to budget your time and money wisely, and seek help from campus resources if needed. Earning a college degree can be a rewarding experience that provides opportunities for personal and professional growth. By starting early, setting realistic goals, focusing on academics, and seeking advice from others, junior high and high school students can prepare for a successful college experience and achieve their goals. Remember to take the college application process one step at a time.

Obtaining the Appropriate Mental Health-Related License

Becoming a licensed mental health professional requires a significant amount of education, training, and experience. However, with dedication and hard work, the process of obtaining a license can be a fulfilling and rewarding experience. The first step is to choose your specialty: Mental health professionals include psychologists, social workers, counselors, and psychiatrists, among others. Each of these professions has different educational and training requirements, so it is important to

     Dr. Roberto Jimenez • *So You Want To Be A Mental Health Professional*

research and choose the one that best aligns with your interests and career goals. Depending on your chosen specialty, you will typically need to complete a graduate program in psychology, social work, counseling, or psychiatry. These programs provide a foundation of knowledge and skills in the field, as well as supervised clinical experience. Many states require mental health professionals to have a certain amount of supervised experience in the field before becoming licensed. This may include completing an internship, working as an assistant, or participating in a residency program.

Most states require mental health professionals to pass a licensing exam, such as the Examination for Professional Practice in Psychology (EPPP), the Association of Social Work Boards (ASWB) exam, or the National Counselor Examination for Licensure and Certification (NCE). These exams test your knowledge and competencies in the field, and must be passed in order to be licensed. After completing the required education and experience, and passing the required exams, you will need to apply for licensure with the state board responsible for licensing mental health professionals. This may involve submitting a license application, proof of education and experience, and a fee. Once you have obtained your license, it is important to maintain it by meeting continuing education requirements, renewing your license periodically, and following ethical standards in your practice. Many states also require mental health professionals to report any disciplinary actions or changes to their status, and to renew their license every few years. Many states require mental health professionals to receive supervision from a licensed professional in their field. This can help you build your skills, gain additional experience, and receive support and guidance in your practice.

Building a network of other mental health professionals can help you stay informed of new developments in the field, find job opportunities, and receive support and guidance in your practice. Consider joining professional organizations, attending conferences, and connecting with other mental health professionals in your area. Once licensed, you can start building your practice by finding clients, setting fees, and promoting your services. Consider developing a niche, such as working with a particular population or using specific therapies, to help differentiate yourself from other mental health professionals. Becoming a licensed mental health professional requires dedication, hard work, and a commitment to continuing education and professional development. By choosing your specialty, completing a graduate program, meeting experience requirements, passing the required exams, and seeking supervision and support, you can obtain a license and build a successful career as a mental health professional.

Additional Guidance

Becoming a mental health professional is a noble and rewarding career choice, but it requires a great deal of dedication, hard work, and education. Here are some additional tips for preparing for a possible career as a mental health professional. The first step is to learn more about the field of mental health. Start by gaining a good understanding of mental health, mental illness, and the various treatments and therapies available. Read books, articles, and research studies, and learn about the different theories and approaches to mental health. Start by reading books and articles about mental health and psychology, both fiction and non-fiction. This will give you a good foundation of knowledge and help you understand the various theories and approaches to mental health. Consider taking psychology and sociology courses in high school, as well as courses that focus on mental health and human development. This will give you a deeper understanding of the field and help you build a strong foundation for further study. Join a club or organization dedicated to mental health, or volunteer at a local mental health organization. This will give you an opportunity to meet and work with mental health professionals, and to learn more about the field. Find a mental health professional who you admire and respect, and ask if they would be willing to mentor you. This will give you an opportunity to learn from someone with experience, and to get their advice and guidance as you pursue your studies. Watching documentaries and films about mental health and psychology can be a great way to learn about the field and to gain a deeper understanding of the issues and challenges faced by those who suffer from mental illness. Participate in online discussions about mental health and psychology by joining online forums and social media groups dedicated to the field. This will give you an opportunity to connect with others who share your interests and to learn from their experiences. There are many online courses and tutorials available that cover topics in mental health and psychology, which can be a great way to gain knowledge and build your skills in the field. Get involved in mental health-related activities. Join a club or organization dedicated to mental health, or volunteer at a local mental health organization. This will give you an opportunity to meet and work with mental health professionals, and to learn more about the field.

Mental health professionals use a wide range of skills, such as active listening, empathy, and communication. Start building these skills now, by volunteering, participating in group activities, and practicing active listening and empathy in your daily life. Stay informed about the latest developments in mental health by reading industry publications, attending conferences and workshops, and participating in continuing education programs. Becoming a mental health professional takes time and dedication, so be patient and persistent.

     Dr. Roberto Jimenez • *So You Want To Be A Mental Health Professional*

Keep your focus on your goal, and continue to build your skills, knowledge, and experience in the field. Mental health work can be emotionally challenging, but it can also be incredibly rewarding. Keep a positive attitude and remember why you chose this path in the first place, and you'll be able to overcome any challenges that come your way. Becoming a mental health professional is a rewarding career choice that requires a strong commitment to education, self-care, and personal growth. If you're willing to work hard, stay focused, and stay informed, you can make a difference in the lives of others and help to improve mental health for all.

Mental health is a crucial aspect of overall well-being, yet it is often neglected and misunderstood. Pursuing a career in mental health can be incredibly rewarding, as mental health professionals play an important role in improving the lives of others. The demand for mental health professionals is on the rise, as mental health issues have become increasingly prevalent in recent years. The World Health Organization (WHO) estimates that one in four people in the world will be affected by mental or neurological disorders at some point in their lives. This growing demand presents a unique opportunity for students to make a significant impact by pursuing a career in mental health.

Mental health professionals help individuals, families, and communities to understand and manage mental health problems. They provide a wide range of services, including therapy, counseling, and support groups. Mental health professionals also play an important role in educating the public about mental health issues and breaking down the stigma surrounding mental illness. A career in mental health offers the opportunity to make a real difference in people's lives. Whether working as a psychologist, counselor, or social worker, mental health professionals have the ability to help individuals manage their mental health issues, overcome obstacles, and achieve their goals. This type of work can be incredibly fulfilling, as mental health professionals are able to see the positive impact they are having on the lives of others.

In addition to the personal fulfillment that comes with a career in mental health, there is also significant potential for professional growth. Mental health professionals have the opportunity to specialize in a particular area, such as child psychology, family therapy, or addiction counseling. They can also continue their education and training throughout their careers, deepening their expertise and expanding their skillset. Pursuing a career in mental health offers the opportunity to make a real difference in the lives of others, as well as personal and professional fulfillment. With the growing demand for mental health professionals and the potential for specialization and growth, a career in mental health is an excellent choice for students who are passionate about helping others and committed to improving mental health for all.

Additional Resources

Below is a list of organizations and agencies that may be of interest to you:

- American Psychological Association (APA)
- National Alliance on Mental Illness (NAMI)
- Substance Abuse and Mental Health Services Administration (SAMHSA)
- National Institute of Mental Health (NIMH)
- Mental Health America
- American Psychiatric Association (APA)
- National Council for Behavioral Health
- Association for Behavioral and Cognitive Therapies (ABCT)
- National Association of Social Workers (NASW)
- American Counseling Association (ACA)
- National Board for Certified Counselors (NBCC)
- International Society for Traumatic Stress Studies (ISTSS)
- National Association of School Psychologists (NASP)
- American School Counselor Association (ASCA)
- International Association of Marriage and Family Counselors (IAMFC)
- American Association of Marriage and Family Therapists (AAMFT)
- American Group Psychotherapy Association (AGPA)
- American Art Therapy Association (AATA)
- American Occupational Therapy Association (AOTA)
- National Association of Cognitive-Behavioral Therapists (NACBT)

Below is a list of internet resources that will provide additional guidance for those interested:

- **American Psychological Association. (2022).** Career Center.
  Retrieved from - https://www.apa.org/careers/resources/career-center

- **National Alliance on Mental Illness. (2023).** Resources for Mental Health Professionals.
  Retrieved from - https://www.nami.org/find-support/professional-resources

- **Substance Abuse and Mental Health Services Administration. (2023).** Workforce Development.
  Retrieved from - https://www.samhsa.gov/workforce/development

- **National Institute of Mental Health. (2023).** Career Information.
  Retrieved from - https://www.nimh.nih.gov/careers/index.shtml

- **Mental Health America. (2023).** Careers in Mental Health.
  Retrieved from - https://www.mentalhealthamerica.net/careers-mental-health

- **American Psychiatric Association. (2023).** Career Center.
  Retrieved from - https://www.psychiatry.org/psychiatrists/career-center

- **National Council for Behavioral Health. (2023).** Career Center.
  Retrieved from - https://www.thenationalcouncil.org/career-center/

- **Association for Behavioral and Cognitive Therapies. (2023).** Career Center.
  Retrieved from - https://www.abct.org/careers/

- **National Association of Social Workers. (2023).** Career Center.
  Retrieved from - https://www.socialworkers.org/careers

- **American Counseling Association. (2023).** Career Center.
  Retrieved from - https://www.counseling.org/careers

- **National Board for Certified Counselors. (2023).** Career Center.
  Retrieved from - https://www.nbcc.org/career-center

- **International Society for Traumatic Stress Studies. (2023).** Career Center. Retrieved from - https://www.istss.org/career-center

- **National Association of School Psychologists. (2023).** Career Center. Retrieved from - https://www.nasponline.org/careers-and-professional-development/career-center

- **American School Counselor Association. (2023).** Career Center. Retrieved from - https://www.schoolcounselor.org/careers

- **International Association of Marriage and Family Counselors. (2023).** Career Center. Retrieved from - https://www.iamfc.org/careers

- **American Association of Marriage and Family Therapists. (2023).** Career Center. Retrieved from - https://www.aamft.org/careers/

- **American Group Psychotherapy Association. (2023).** Career Center. Retrieved from - https://www.agpa.org/careers

- **American Art Therapy Association. (2023).** Career Center. Retrieved from - https://www.arttherapy.org/careers

- **American Occupational Therapy Association. (2023).** Career Center. Retrieved from - https://www.aota.org/careers.aspx

- **National Association of Cognitive-Behavioral Therapists. (2023).** Career Center. Retrieved from - https://www.nacbt.org/careers

References

- **American Art Therapy Association. (2023).** Career Center. Retrieved from - https://www.arttherapy.org/careers

- **American Association of Marriage and Family Therapists. (2023).** Career Center. Retrieved from - https://www.aamft.org/careers/

- **American Counseling Association. (2023).** Career Center. Retrieved from - https://www.counseling.org/careers

- **American Group Psychotherapy Association. (2023).** Career Center. Retrieved from - https://www.agpa.org/careers

- **American Occupational Therapy Association. (2023).** Career Center. Retrieved from - https://www.aota.org/careers.aspx

- **American Psychological Association. (2022).** Career Center. Retrieved from - https://www.apa.org/careers/resources/career-center

- **American Psychiatric Association. (2023).** Career Center. Retrieved from - https://www.psychiatry.org/psychiatrists/career-center

- **American School Counselor Association. (2023).** Career Center. Retrieved from - https://www.schoolcounselor.org/careers

- **Association for Behavioral and Cognitive Therapies. (2023).** Career Center. Retrieved from - https://www.abct.org/careers/

- **International Society for Traumatic Stress Studies. (2023).** Career Center. Retrieved from - https://www.istss.org/career-center

- **International Association of Marriage and Family Counselors. (2023).** Career Center. Retrieved from - https://www.iamfc.org/careers

- **Mental Health America. (2023).** Careers in Mental Health. Retrieved from - https://www.mentalhealthamerica.net/careers-mental-health

- **National Alliance on Mental Illness. (2023).** Resources for Mental Health Professionals.
  Retrieved from - https://www.nami.org/find-support/professional-resources

- **National Association of Cognitive-Behavioral Therapists. (2023).** Career Center.
  Retrieved from - https://www.nacbt.org/careers

- **National Association of Social Workers. (2023).** Career Center.
  Retrieved from - https://www.socialworkers.org/careers

- **National Association of School Psychologists. (2023).** Career Center.
  Retrieved from - https://www.nasponline.org/careers-and-professional-development/career-center

- **Substance Abuse and Mental Health Services Administration. (2023).** Workforce Development.
  Retrieved from - https://www.samhsa.gov/workforce/development

- **National Board for Certified Counselors. (2023).** Career Center.
  Retrieved from - https://www.nbcc.org/career-center

- **National Council for Behavioral Health. (2023).** Career Center.
  Retrieved from - https://www.thenationalcouncil.org/career-center/

- **National Institute of Mental Health. (2023).** Career Information.
  Retrieved from - https://www.nimh.nih.gov/careers/index.shtml

www.ingramcontent.com/pod-product-compliance
Lightning Source LLC
Chambersburg PA
CBHW041952130726
48010CB00022B/172

9 798987 622858